imagine
yesterday...today

International garden and landscape photography

imagine
yesterday...today

International garden and landscape photography

Kew
PLANTS PEOPLE
POSSIBILITIES

GPA
GARDEN PHOTOGRAPHERS ASSOCIATION
Part of the Garden Writers' Guild

THIRD MILLENNIUM
PUBLISHING, LONDON III

Imagine yesterday...today

First published in 2006 by Third Millennium Publishing Ltd,
a subsidiary of Third Millennium Information Ltd

2–5 Benjamin Street
London
EC1M 5QL
www.tmiltd.com

Garden Photographers' Association Exhibition 2006
Imagine yesteray...today
Organiser: Helen Fickling
Edited by: Henrietta Van den Bergh and Helen Fickling

Designed and produced by Third Millennium Publishing
Printed and bound in Italy by Printer Trento

Printed on GardaMatt Art 150 gsm, ECF, produced with cellulose coming
from certified or well managed forests or plantations.

ISBN 10 : 1 903942 57 8
ISBN 13 : 978 1 903942 57 4

Front cover:
Stone Pine, David Steel

Back cover:
TL: Waterlily Display, Derek Harris
TR: Backlit Poppy Seed Head, Rowan Isaac
BR: Winter Pagoda, Jeff Eden
BL: Rhubarb Pickers, Jonathan Buckley

Frontispiece:
Picasso of Trees, Andrea Jones

Imprint page:
Useless Trees, Eduard Popescu

Contents

Bad Hair Day, Andrew Butler

Foreword

It is a great pleasure to welcome to the Royal Botanic Gardens, Kew, for a second time, a wonderful exhibition organised and presented by the Garden Photographers' Association – and on a theme that is central to what Kew is, and what Kew does. This collection of superb images – almost one hundred are illustrated in this beautiful book – takes the overarching theme of 'heritage' at its most expansive. But at the very centre is the notion of maintaining and sustaining those special places, both close to home and far away, that link us to plants, to our history and to our future. The images in this book show us that the six billion plus people alive on the planet today have inherited a world that is still wonderfully rich in natural and cultural resources of almost unimaginable diversity. But they also remind us that it will be the actions of all of us, especially in the next few decades, that will determine the nature of the inheritance that we will pass on to our children and grandchildren.

This book, and the exhibition that it accompanies, brings together stunning images from Britain and around the world by a hugely talented group of photographers. Two of the four categories focus on gardens in the very broad sense: those that are still sustained largely by the processes of nature, and those created more directly by our own interventions and imaginations. Today, the whole of our planet is a garden, influenced everywhere – to a greater or lesser degree – by our own pervasive presence.

Two other categories focus on those remarkable places, Kew among them, that are truly extraordinary and of outstanding universal value from the standpoint of nature, or culture, or both. If there were ever any doubt, these images show us just how much we have to lose if we neglect our responsibility for careful stewardship. Taken together, the images across all four categories could scarcely be more diverse, but they also pose the same two simple, recurrent, questions. How did these places come into existence? And what will be their future?

All of us at the Royal Botanic Gardens, Kew are grateful to Helen Fickling, Henrietta Van den Bergh and the exhibition team from the Garden Photographers' Association for assembling such a splendid collection of works for this book and for the exhibition. I am delighted that once again we can host such an original and magnificent show at Kew. On behalf of the tens of thousands of visitors who will visit the exhibition and enjoy these images, it is my very great pleasure to thank all the contributors. We marvel at their skill in connecting us to places of great beauty and great significance, but we also appreciate the opportunity to share their personal perspectives in a way that helps us reflect on our natural and cultural heritage – and what its future should be.

Professor Sir Peter R. Crane FRS
Director
Royal Botanic Gardens, Kew

Acknowledgements

08 The Garden Photographers' Association (GPA) offer their
sincerest gratitude and thanks to Helen Fickling, Martin Page,
Henrietta Van den Bergh, Robert Whitworth and the many
individuals, in particular Andrew Fickling, who have given their
time, expertise and assistance in making the exhibition and
publication possible. In addition, the GPA wish to express a
very special thank you to Third Millennium Publishing for
producing this publication, the third in the series.

We also extend our grateful thanks to the Royal Botanic
Gardens, Kew for their unfailing enthusiasm and support, and
to our judges who selected the images for the exhibition.

A special thank you also goes to our exhibition sponsors for
their valued support.

Introduction

Henrietta Van den Bergh and Helen Fickling

Nature's gardens, nurtured gardens, and UNESCO World Heritage sites from around the world feature in this year's Garden Photographers' Association exhibition, *Imagine yesterday…today*. Based on an overall theme of 'Heritage', over 900 images were entered, each of which was viewed by an independent panel of judges, resulting in a final selection of 98 images chosen for exhibition. As one of the judges, Jess Walton, said: 'It never ceases to amaze me how a single subject matter can be interpreted in so many different ways, from the adventurous to the humorous and from the simple to the complex.' And we are confident that you will be equally surprised and enchanted.

The Garden Photographers' Association (previously known as the Garden Photographers' Group) joined the Garden Writers' Guild in 2000, thus providing a forum in which to address issues within the horticultural community and to stimulate creativity amongst its members and associated professionals. The group continues to have an active international membership, many of whom are major contributors to the horticultural media worldwide.

The Guild was established in 1991 as the national organisation for professional communicators associated with the horticultural community. Membership includes writers, broadcasters, photographers, artists and illustrators, along with book, magazine and newspaper publishers.

Theme and Categories

Imagine yesterday…today's 'Heritage' theme was designed to challenge photographers' imagination. Heritage includes the things we want to keep – places, environments and objects that have aesthetic, historic, scientific or social meaning, or a special value that may give us a sense of the past. Such places or objects may have cultural significance for a particular group or community in our society, which each wishes to protect and pass on to future generations.

In all categories we looked for emotive imagery, broad views or intimate details that capture the imagination and record a moment in time. Images that address both social and political issues that are relevant to our heritage today, or that incorporate an element of education, protection or prevention, whether reflecting the past or the future. We wanted photographers to consider the passing of time, the effects of seasonal and climatic change. The theme was set to explore our 'heritage' in its widest sense, including the role plants have played, and gave photographers the challenge of capturing its essence by showing a sense of place within four categories.

Nature's Garden – *gardens created by nature*

This category encouraged entrants to capture natural garden environments worldwide. For example, woodlands and forests, grasslands, coastal regions, deserts, moors, bogs, mountains and so on. It is all about raw nature and the totally natural gardens that surround us, the stories our landscapes tell and the positive or negative impact mankind has had on them. The flora and fauna that live within these natural habitats should all have been considered, along with the effects of seasonal and climatic change and the passing of time. We were not looking for pure wildlife or people images, and any inclusion of these should have been incidental to the environment in which they were found.

Nurtured Gardens – *gardens created by man*

Entrants were encouraged to submit images of gardens and environments created, built and nurtured by man, both past and present. The gardens we create for social pleasure and enjoyment are influenced by culture and are a testament to who we are. They are a labour of love. They reflect on yesteryear and look to the future, incorporating fashion and fads, traditions and skills handed down from generation to generation, some of which have almost become an art form.

Private and public gardens, parks and other public spaces, palaces, stately homes and their gardens, monuments and follies, urban environments, biodiversity and the influence of technology were all to be considered, as well as why, for what purpose and how man's environments were created. This was not about agriculture and industry but rather the garden, a place of work and play, in its various manmade forms. Images could include all the elements that man has used to create his special places and illustrate the time and effort he has dedicated to protecting the plants within them.

Royal Botanic Gardens, Kew – *a UNESCO World Heritage site*

Under this category we were looking for inspiring and stunning imagery of the structures and features within the Royal Botanic Gardens, Kew, Surrey, UK. These could be anything within the gardens from 200-year-old heritage trees, close-up details of a plant or groups of plants and studies of the historical buildings to the many magnificent panoramic vistas and focal points found in this 300-acre UNESCO World Heritage site. The images should depict not only Kew's historical elements, but also what Kew means to us today – its work on conservation and awareness, its festivals, the people who work there, and how it's used and enjoyed.

World Heritage Sites – *those protected and those that should be*

This category brings together the essence of both nature's gardens and nurtured gardens at the 812 UNESCO World Heritage sites worldwide.

We were looking for personal interpretations of World Heritage sites, their buildings and artifacts, the space around them, whether natural or manmade, and specifically how they relate to one another. The sites and their surroundings from a botanical perspective were to be considered as well as the effect of seasonal and climatic change and the influences that man has had on them. Here we were not looking for pure architecture, cityscapes or industrial landscapes, but rather interpretations of spaces within, and the importance of, these World Heritage sites and their symbolism in terms of environments created and thereafter protected by UNESCO.

Entries and Judging

The call for entries was placed with photographic magazines and associations, photographic retail outlets and laboratories, the exhibition website and other related websites. As a result, over 900 entries were received from around the world, with images shot in Argentina, Australia, Belgium, Canada, Chile, Guatemala, Japan, Finland, Russia, South Africa, Namibia, Spain, the USA and, not least, the UK.

On Tuesday 7 and Wednesday 8 March, the Royal Botanic Gardens, Kew hosted the judging. All images were judged anonymously and were chosen for their technical and artistic merit, and their interpretation of the theme and categories.

Judges

James Alexander-Sinclair – Garden Designer, Writer and TV Presenter, Northamptonshire, UK
Joe Cornish – Landscape Photographer, London, UK
Rasshied Din – Design Consultant, Din Associates, London, UK
Laura Giuffrida – Exhibition and Live Interpretations Manager, Royal Botanic Gardens, Kew, Surrey, UK

Michael Hoppen – Michael Hoppen Gallery, London, UK
Juliet Roberts – Editor, Gardens Illustrated Magazine, Bristol, UK
Jess Walton – Creative Visual Research, London, UK

Awards and Prizes
The winners of *Imagine yesterday...today* were announced at the exhibition launch event on 24 May, at White Peaks, Royal Botanic Gardens, Kew where the exhibition was officially opened and the awards were presented.

OVERALL WINNER:
Nicola Browne – Poplars
A Timber Merchant's Garden, near Antwerp, Belgium

Nature's Garden
Best of Category: Richard Freestone: Grass Seeds (The Next Generation 2), Derby, Derbyshire, England, UK
Second: Allan Pollock-Morris: Moonlight Sonata Helmingham Hall, Suffolk, England, UK
Third: Steve Gallagher: Winter at Mayhill Gloucestershire, England, UK

Nurtured Gardens
Best of Category: Nicola Browne: Poplars
A Timber Merchant's Garden, near Antwerp, Belgium
Second: Andrea Jones: Picasso of Trees Hither Lane, Long Island, USA
Third: Carol Sharp: Wild Tulip Duet – *Tulipa acuminita* RHS Chelsea Flower Show, London, England, UK

Royal Botanic Gardens, Kew
Best of Category: Nadia Mackenzie: *Agave* Royal Botanic Gardens, Kew, Surrey, England, UK
Second: Derek St Romaine: Ancient Tools Royal Botanic Gardens, Kew, Surrey, England, UK

Third: Marcus Foster: Gulls Seeking Winter Warmth Royal Botanic Gardens, Kew, Surrey, England, UK

World Heritage Sites
Best of Category: Jill Furmanovsky: Roman Road to Glastonbury Tor, Somerset, England, UK
Second: Peter Mason: Orchid Beach, Fraser Island, Queensland, Australia
Third: Andrew Butler: Studley Royal Water Garden (National Trust), Ripon, North Yorkshire, England, UK

Judges' Favourites
• Nicola Browne – Poplars
  A Timber Merchant's Garden, near Antwerp, Belgium
• Jonathan Buckley, Rhubarb Pickers
  Wakefield, Yorkshire, England, UK
• Andrea Jones, Picasso of Trees, Hither Lane, Long Island, USA
• Nadia Mackenzie, *Agave*, Royal Botanic Gardens, Kew, Surrey, England, UK
• Nadege Meriau, Pond in Finland, near Pori, Satakunta, Finland
• Allan Pollock-Morris, Oak Avenue, Keepers Cottage, Helmingham Hall, Suffolk, England, UK

All photographers should be encouraged to explore new techniques and to push their creativity. With the competition, the Garden Photographers' Association aims to provide a challenge for professional, assistant, student and aspiring photographers and an opportunity for them to promote themselves through their work, particularly as a fine art form, at the exhibition.

For more information on the exhibition, please visit:
www.gpoty.com

or email:
Helen Fickling: exhibition06@garden-photographers.com
Martin Page: press06@garden-photographers.com

Grass Speared Leaf, Mike Curry

Heritage through a Lens

Tim Smit, CEO and co-founder of The Eden Project

If you can't drink in them, can't dream in them and don't feel like making love in them – tarmac them. This should be the guiding principle of restoration and conservation. The pious library-toned language that accompanies the word 'heritage' makes me want to scream. It is not exclusively a British trait, but the British are the world leaders. Every garden and house over a certain age is deemed important, unique or vital in its designation, when the subtext should be 'we're scared of the future and the past is obviously a better place'. It is a place of thatched cottages with smoke billowing out of every chimney and a happy family frolicking and the smell of bread in the air.

There is nothing better or more romantic than walking through a fine garden or landscape. Who can resist the sheer joy of a beautiful herbaceous border whether designed by Gertrude Jekyll or Christopher Lloyd? Who doesn't feel the slightly menacing presence of Mr McGregor and the thrill of being Peter Rabbit in a burgeoning vegetable garden? Who isn't transported into bodice-ripping imagination at Stourhead? Who can fail to be entranced by a 500-year-old tree in an ancient forest? Great gardens and landscapes are beautiful, powerful things, and at their best capture every emotion from pure wonder, through melancholy, to romance and monastic serenity. When offered the choice between a visit to a previously unsampled pub and a new garden, a great friend, an internationally recognised plantsman, once memorably said: 'I shall know all the plants, albeit they will be in a different order – let's go to the pub!' A great garden isn't about plants you see, it's about atmosphere. Just like a great painting isn't about paint, or even the technique of its application. No, great gardens have an almost spiritual quality.

Their value lies purely in whether they provide pleasure. Roy Strong once observed, 'the gardens that have most moved me have been redolent of the character of their makers or resonant with some huge idea'. I couldn't improve on that.

Having said that a great garden isn't about plants, the opposite is also self-evidently true. The explosion of plants brought to Britain by the great plant hunters have been discussed in dozens of books and we owe them, their mentors and the great institutions that managed the process a huge debt for giving us the most glorious palette with which to play. Here in Cornwall, where we have the most clement of climates, the great gardens are a testament to that. Tresco, Chyverton, Trewithen, Glendurgan are masterpieces of plant confection. Garden visiting is at an all time high, and it is hard to escape the ubiquitous presence and commentary of our most famous garden designers and plantsmen, whether it be on television, the radio or in magazines and glossy books. But, something is happening that marks a huge change. While we still marvel at these great living tableaux and the great landscapists who moved hillsides and lawns, dug lakes and rivers, hewed waterfalls and rock gardens on an extraordinary scale, to create their own versions of Eden, the responses are changing. The heritage factor is wearing out and 'meaning' is creeping in. Britain boasts landscapes and gardens both formal and informal that are, without argument, the finest in the world. The designers of them rank with the greatest of artists, anywhere. The pleasure they bring is immeasurable, and their role in framing a view of the brand that is UK plc is so large as to be unquantifiable but….

14 The great gardens and designed landscapes are, by and large, exercises in the defiance of nature. The designer improves on what nature has offered up and sets to work creating a picture, more pleasing, more natural that will perfectly set off the house of the patron, offering vistas, plantings and site lines that confirm not only his wealth and power (I say he, for most patrons were men), but most importantly, his sophistication and taste. The greatest crime would be to exhibit parochialism and thus admit that one had not often been in 'town' or made the Grand Tour.

In 2003 Tessa Traeger and Patrick Kinmonth produced a book of photographs and interviews that formed a major exhibition at the National Portrait Gallery entitled *A Gardener's Labyrinth: Portraits of People, Plants and Places*, which was superbly constructed as a work in five movements featuring commentary by some of the finest exponents of the garden craft: The Garden Proposed; The Garden Described; The Garden Planted (featuring the blue-ribbon plantsmen and women); The Garden Preserved and, lastly, The Garden Explored. The photographs were superb and works of art in their own right, but what struck me particularly strongly was that they chronicled a significant shift that had taken place over a very short period of time, from self-deprecation to self-expression. The new breed of commentators and plantsmen, while respectful of the past, seemed to be breathing the heady air of liberty. The straightjacket of historic correctness, heritage in aspic, was unknotting. No babies were being thrown out with the bathwater, but everywhere one could see gardeners and garden owners exploring the fullest potential of their gardens. The past five years have seen a steady growth in interest at what is on offer at the great shows at Chelsea, Hampton Court, Tatton Park and elsewhere, and a huge growth in interest from the general public in gardening in general. Garden writing and photography are now firmly classified under 'culture'!

Something profound is happening which I haven't seen described. I recognised early on at Heligan that people were deeply moved by the gentle melancholy of its walled gardens and fantastically overgrown pleasure grounds. They were moved to sadness by the human story of the gardeners who went to war and never came back and they were in awe at the power of nature, in no time at all, to regain its hold on all that had been nurtured. What was it in people's eyes as they surveyed the vegetables growing? Was there something very primitive here, a folk memory, the distant rumour of the hunter gatherer in us? I can't say, but you see it at The Eden Project too, the long pause and the momentarily distant look as the Arcadian wild is broken by small islands of domestication. The look is childlike. Gardens are about many things and they are highly individual, but as we become ever more urbanised they take on a symbolic power. Working in a garden becomes somehow an affirmation that we are part of, not apart from nature. That our efforts to control the perceived danger of the wild by creating glades of tranquillity are in fact a silent scream; we are alive – and scared of dying.

Pretentious stuff? Why then is the profile of the amateur gardener now becoming so varied in both demography and background of the participants? Why do the public lap up the photographs of Andrew Lawson, Tessa Traeger, Hugh Palmer, Andrea Jones and the dozens of others I could mention? Their work has changed too. The shots of gardens in bloom have taken on a much richer colour and mood, of tunnels and avenues, of nature closely observed, sexual and feral, decay and rebirth, and yet wondrous, as if the structures are being viewed for the very first time. The imagery of such works as the Diary of an Edwardian Country Lady is giving way to photo essays that capture mood. Is it a coincidence then that our great horticultural institutions, the Royal Botanic Gardens at Kew and Edinburgh, the Royal Horticultural Society, the National Trust and many of the great gardens are enjoying a renaissance in visitor numbers? Is it a coincidence that over the last few years they have all moved mountains to shed the baggage of their collective pasts in order to become outward-looking organisations responding to the new current of interest in plants, gardens and by association the livelihoods dependent on them. You could call it almost a spiritual hunger. Whether it be the

scientific world's resurgent interest in biomimetics or consumers' embrace of all things organic, there is something going on.

It is interesting that as you walk round the Great Palm House at Kew and listen to people talking, while the imperial ambitions that saw its creation have long gone, those same collections, once seen as jewels of empire, are being talked of as the wealth and hope of humankind. That is a significant journey. Similar new points of reference are to be overheard at many great gardens, where the hushed tones of reverence are replaced by laughter and picnics, and new traditions for their enjoyment are being created, with events and artistic interventions to make them relevant to today. Music in the Park? We go every year, it's a tradition. Funny stuff heritage, we can't get enough of it and for some strange reason I think we have just begun a new journey which will leave a very different inheritance seen through a very different lens.

Our England is a garden that is full of stately views,

Of borders, beds and shrubberies and lawns and avenues,

With statues on the terraces and peacocks strutting by;

But the Glory of the Garden lies in more than meets the eye.

RUDYARD KIPLING

EXTRACT TAKEN FROM THE GLORY OF THE GARDEN

Scotney Castle Gardens (National Trust)
Andrew Butler

Lamberhurst, Kent, England, UK
Colour transparency shot on Canham DLC45

Nurtured Gardens

Winter in Powerscourt Gardens
George Munday

Powerscourt Gardens, County Wicklow, Ireland
Colour transparency shot on Mamiya RZ67

Nurtured Gardens

The Farm Pond
Charlie Hopkinson

Sussex, England, UK
Polaroid film shot on NPC land camera

Nature's Garden

20

Lone Tree, Limestone and Last Light
David Tarn

Twisleton Scar, Ingleborough, Yorkshire, England, UK
Colour transparency shot on Ebony 45S

Nature's Garden

All Year Round
Andrea Jones

Private Garden of Ian Sidaway, Strawberry Hill,
Twickenham, Surrey, England, UK
Digital image shot on Kodak DCS Pro 14n

Nurtured Gardens

22

Arrowhead Foliage
Andrew Butler

Royal Botanic Gardens,
Kew, Surrey, England, UK
Digital image shot on Nikon D70

Royal Botanic Gardens, Kew

Prairie Planting at Lady Farm
Andrew Lawson

Lady Farm, Chelwood, Somerset, England, UK
Colour transparency shot on Hasselblad XPan

Nurtured Gardens

24

Mystical Wistman's Wood
Derek Harris

Dartmoor, Devon, England, UK
Colour transparency shot on Fuji GW690

Nature's Garden

The Exotic Garden
Jonathan Buckley

Great Dixter, Rye, East Sussex, England, UK
Digital image shot on Kodak DCS Pro 14n

Nurtured Gardens

Frosted Fungi
John Martin

Coombe Abbey Country Park, near Coventry, England, UK
Colour transparency shot on Minolta Dynax 9

Nature's Garden

Magnolia in Spring
Nadege Meriau

Royal Botanic Gardens, Kew, Surrey, England, UK
Colour negative shot on Hasselblad 500CM

Royal Botanic Gardens, Kew

Judge's Favourite

Joe Cornish
Landscape Photographer, UK

At first glance this photograph of an agave might elicit the response that it was simply a very fine plant portrait. But the longer I looked at it the more I fell in love with its perfect proportions and beautifully balanced sense of energy. Strange to relate, the colour green, in all its myriad hues, is one of the hardest of nature's colours to capture satisfactorily. Yet this image does so, every subtle nuance of the agave's surface being perfectly reproduced.

Lighting and composition are crucial to me, and indeed are vital in most aspects of photographing the natural world. Whether a plant is wild or propagated it should be lit sensitively to reveal its structure and shape. And the photographer needs to adopt precisely the right camera position, perspective and lens focal length to both reveal its form, and to exclude what is unnecessary or distracting.

There is no need for forced originality here. This picture is simply an outstanding example of doing everything right. The photograph's perfection allows the plant to live within the frame, to be both still and dynamic, making it for me much more than just another plant portrait. I wish I had done it!

Agave
Nadia Mackenzie

Royal Botanic Gardens, Kew, Surrey, England, UK
Colour transparency shot on Canon F-1

Royal Botanic Gardens, Kew
Judge's Favourite

30

The Temperate House
Jeff Eden

Royal Botanic Gardens, Kew, Surrey, England, UK
Colour transparency shot on Nikon FM2

Royal Botanic Gardens, Kew

Moonlight Sonata ②
Allan Pollock-Morris

Helmingham Hall, Suffolk, England, UK
Digital image shot on Nikon D2X

Nature's Garden

Winter Pagoda
Jeff Eden

Royal Botanic Gardens, Kew, Surrey, England, UK
Black and white negative shot on Nikon FM2

Royal Botanic Gardens, Kew

White Orchid
Anne Green-Armytage

Royal Botanic Gardens, Kew, Surrey, England, UK
Digital image shot on Canon EOS-1Ds Mark II

Royal Botanic Gardens, Kew

Purple Invitation
Liz Eddison

Royal Botanic Gardens, Kew, Surrey, England, UK
Colour transparency shot on Nikon FM3a

Royal Botanic Gardens, Kew

Waterlily Display
Derek Harris

Royal Botanic Gardens, Kew, Surrey, England, UK
Colour transparency shot on Fuji GW690

Royal Botanic Gardens, Kew

Rhubarb Pickers
Jonathan Buckley

Wakefield, Yorkshire, England, UK
Digital image shot on Kodak DCS Pro 14n

Nurtured Gardens
Judge's Favourite

Judge's Favourite

James Alexander-Sinclair
Garden Designer, Writer and TV Presenter, UK

Picking a favourite from so many outstanding photographs seemed terribly daunting at first, but every time I wandered off I was drawn back by the siren song of one image so, in the end, it was a doddle.

On the surface it is all about forced rhubarb (which needs to be grown in the dark and picked by candlelight). It is a portrait of three men bent double in a dark tunnel picking armfuls of pallid rhubarb, their backs straining, the fruit cold on their forearms, and the sunlight a distant memory – hard work.

Alternatively, the imagination can be goaded towards a much more romantic interpretation: the cold catacomb becomes a hushed cathedral, the pickers are transformed into genuflecting acolytes and the sticks of rhubarb become devotional candles dripping wax.

Industry, spirituality, light, imagination and rhubarb (with the promise of crumble!).

Wild at Heart #2
Dianna Jazwinski

Chesil Beach, Dorset, England, UK
Colour transparency shot on Canon EOS-1N

Nature's Garden

Grass Speared Leaf
Mike Curry

The New Forest, Hampshire, England, UK
Digital image shot on Olympus E-1

Nature's Garden

40

Orchid
Nadia Mackenzie

Royal Botanic Gardens, Kew, Surrey, England, UK
Digital image shot on Nikon N70

Royal Botanic Gardens, Kew

Dawn at Dead Vlei
Jeff Overs

Soussesvlei, Namibia, Africa
Digital image shot on Nikon D100

Nature's Garden

Behind the Scenes at the Waterlily House
Sharon Pearson

Royal Botanic Gardens, Kew, Surrey, England, UK
Digital image shot on Canon EOS 5D

Royal Botanic Gardens, Kew

Fade
Richard Adkin

Mosteiro dos Capuchos, Sintra, Lisbon, Portugal
Colour transparency shot on Canon EOS ELAN II

World Heritage Sites

Jess Walton
Creative Visual Research, UK

The composition of this image is simply wonderful, with the winding track echoed by the avenue of trees that leads us through to some unknown but intriguing place beyond. It has such a beautiful light emphasising the stillness and freshness of the early morning. A magical moment captured by the photographer – don't you just want to be there?

2 **Picasso of Trees**
Andrea Jones

Hither Lane, Long Island, USA
Colour transparency shot on Mamiya RB67

Nurtured Gardens
Judge's Favourite

46

Light Dawns
Andrea Jones

San Juan and Quetzaltenango, Guatemala
Digital image shot on Kodak DCS Pro 14n

Nature's Garden

Canna **'Ra' in the Temperate House**
Sara Barraud

Royal Botanic Gardens, Kew, Surrey, England, UK
Digital image shot on Canon-1Ds Mark II

Royal Botanic Gardens, Kew

Here Comes the Sun
Andrea Jones

Napa Valley, California, USA
Colour transparency shot on Fuji Panoramic GX 617

Nature's Garden

Southern Beech and Glacier
Kevin Schafer

Perito Mereno Glacier, Los Glaciares National Park,
Patagonia, Argentina
Colour transparency shot on Nikon F100

World Heritage Sites

50

Aloe
Nadia Mackenzie

Royal Botanic Gardens, Kew, Surrey, England, UK
Colour transparency shot on Canon F-1

Royal Botanic Gardens, Kew

A Pavlovsk Winter
Clive Nichols

Pavlovsk Palace, Pavlovsk Park, near St Petersburg, Russia
Colour transparency shot on Nikon F90X

Nurtured Gardens

1 Roman Road to Glastonbury Tor
Jill Furmanovsky

Somerset, England, UK
Colour negative shot on Nikon F5

World Heritage Sites

The willow
is smart
in a suit
of yellow

E. NESBIT

EXTRACT FROM CHILD'S SONG IN SPRING

Willow Tree
Nadege Meriau

Mother's Garden, Héric, Loire-Atlantique, France
Colour negative shot on Hasselblad 500CM

Nurtured Gardens

120 Seconds
Paul Debois

Royal Botanic Gardens, Kew, Surrey, England, UK
Digital image shot on Kodak DCS Pro SLR/c

Royal Botanic Gardens, Kew

58

Unplanned Garden
Nikki de Gruchy

Private Garden, Andalucia, Spain
Colour transparency shot on Hasselblad 501CM

Nature's Garden

Penny Bridge
Andrew Butler

Exmoor, England, UK
Colour transparency shot on Canham DLC45

Nature's Garden

Seaweed on Rocks at Low Tide
Rob Whitworth

Lizard Peninsular, Cornwall, England, UK
Colour transparency shot on Bronica ETR-Si

Nature's Garden

Recreating Nature
John Garrett

Covent Garden, London, England, UK
Black and white negative shot on Nikon F90X

Nurtured Gardens

Backlit Poppy Seed Head
Rowan Isaac

Winterbourne Down, Bristol, England, UK
Digital image shot on Nikon D70

Nurtured Gardens

Gulls Seeking Winter Warmth ❸
Marcus Foster

Royal Botanic Gardens, Kew, Surrey, England, UK
Colour transparency shot on Pentax ME SUPER

Royal Botanic Gardens, Kew

64

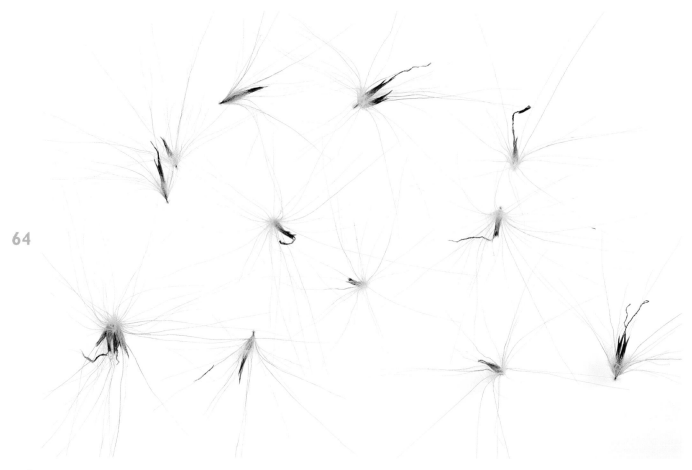

① Grass Seeds (The Next Generation 2)
Richard Freestone

Derby, Derbyshire, England, UK
Digital image shot on Canon-1Ds Mark II

Nature's Garden

The Workers
Helen Fickling

Royal Botanic Gardens, Kew, Surrey, England, UK
Colour transparency shot on Mamiya RZ67 Pro 2

Royal Botanic Gardens, Kew

Judge's Favourite

Rasshied Din
Design Consultant, Din Associates, UK

I was greatly impressed by this particular picture as it is a very powerful image. It has many qualities, it's very minimal, and almost painterly in quality. The image is of an abstract nature, and almost architectural in its strength and power. The relationship and proximity of the trees draws you into the picture, and it makes one feel that there is a magical quality to this place, a real sense of enchantment. The image also has a graphic linear quality, with a richness of colour, texture, and composition. The play of sunshine and shade really draws you into the frame, and the fingering shadows of the trees almost seem to be reaching out of the picture and enticing you into this enchanted world.

Juliet Roberts
Editor, Gardens Illustrated Magazine, UK

This photograph stood out for its uncomplicated drama. The simplicity of the subject matter combines with the image's painterly quality to make it timeless and serene. I particularly like how the verticality of the poplar trees is emphasised by the angle at which it was shot, with golden sunshine in the middle distance creating shadows over the brightly lit grass beneath. The eye is drawn by the stark geometry of the tree trunks, which is further underscored by the horizontal plane of the hedge beyond. I find the intense clarity of the greens contrasts with the blackness of the trunks, giving a purity and elegance to the composition. An intensely haunting image that stays with you long after you've stopped gazing at it.

OVERALL WINNER
Poplars ❶
Nicola Browne

A Timber Merchant's Garden, near Antwerp, Belgium
Colour transparency shot on Nikon F100

Nurtured Gardens
Judge's Favourite

Steps and Stone Balls
Rowan Isaac

St Fagans, Cardiff, Wales, UK
Colour transparency shot on Hasselblad 500CM

Nurtured Gardens

Papaver somniferum
Rob Whitworth

Goulters Mill Garden, Wiltshire, England, UK
Colour transparency shot on Hasselblad XPan II

Nurtured Gardens

Reeds
Henrietta Van den Bergh

Greater St Lucia Wetland Park, Kwa-Zulu Natal, South Africa
Colour transparency shot on Canon F-1

World Heritage Sites

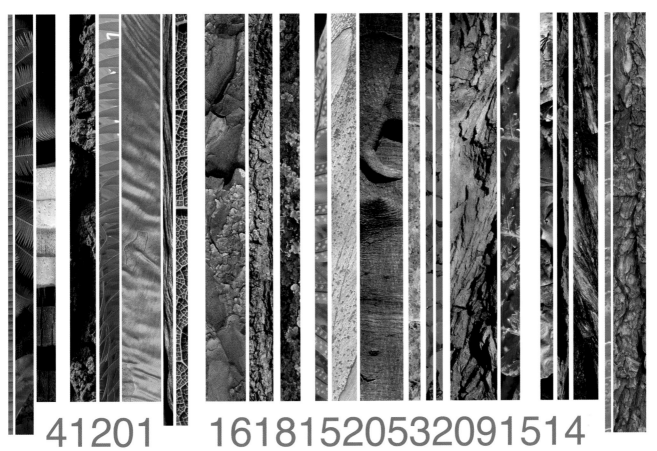

41201 16181520532091514

Data Protection
Helen Fickling

Various locations worldwide
Colour transparency shot on Nikon F3

Nature's Garden

A Living Patchwork
Lindsey Stock

Royal Botanic Gardens, Kew, Surrey, England, UK
Digital image shot on Kodak DCS Pro 14n

Royal Botanic Gardens, Kew

The Bottle Palm
Sara Barraud

Royal Botanic Gardens, Kew, Surrey, England, UK
Digital image shot on Canon-1Ds Mark II

Royal Botanic Gardens, Kew

74

Pettifers Winter
Clive Nichols

Pettifers, Lower Wardington, Oxfordshire, England, UK
Colour transparency shot on Pentax 67

Nurtured Gardens

Outside Looking In
Sara Barraud

Royal Botanic Gardens, Kew, Surrey, England, UK
Digital image shot on Canon-1Ds Mark II

Royal Botanic Gardens, Kew

Derek Jarman's Garden
Robert Bird

Dungeness, Kent, England, UK
Digital image shot on Nikon D70

Nurtured Gardens

Nant Gwynant Valley
Jason Ingram

Llyn Gwynant and the Nant, Gwynant Valley, Snowdonia, Wales, UK
Black and white negative shot on Mamiya TLR C330S

Nature's Garden

78

Teasels
Dianna Jazwinski

Studland Beach and Nature Reserve, Dorset, England, UK
Black and white film shot on Canon EOS 600

Nature's Garden

Elephant Ear *(Colocasia esculenta)*
Nadia Mackenzie

Royal Botanic Gardens, Kew, Surrey, England, UK
Colour transparency shot on Canon F-1

Royal Botanic Gardens, Kew

Urn at Dawn
Steve Bicknell

Royal Botanic Gardens, Kew, Surrey, England, UK
Digital image shot on Canon EOS-1Ds Mark 1

Royal Botanic Gardens, Kew

Studley Royal Water Garden (National Trust) 3
Andrew Butler

Ripon, North Yorkshire, England, UK
Colour transparency shot on Canham DLC45

World Heritage Sites

Wheelbarrows at Hill Close Gardens
Rob Whitworth

Hill Close Gardens, Warwickshire, England, UK
Colour transparency shot on Hasselblad XPan II

Nurtured Gardens

The Gardener
John Garrett

Chiswick Allotments, London, England, UK
Black and white negative shot on Nikon F90X

Nurtured Gardens

84

Dry Stream Bed
Paul Green

Sapperton Valley Nature Reserve, Gloucestershire, England, UK
Polaroid shot on Arca Swiss 5x4 F-Line View Camera

Nature's Garden

Spiralling
Liz Eddison

Royal Botanic Gardens, Kew, Surrey, England, UK
Colour transparency shot on Nikon FM3a

Royal Botanic Gardens, Kew

Judge's Favourite

Laura Giuffrida
Exhibition and Live Interpretations Manager,
Royal Botanic Gardens, Kew, UK

This small, dark, potent photograph immediately intrigued me. Through the avenue of ancient oaks, casting their velvet black moonlit shadows on the pathway, leading me to a distant glowing light – I am transported to the world of Jane Austen, Wilkie Collins, or even Lawrence's Lady Chatterley!

This is a rich, mysterious, enfolding image, evocative of an early Samuel Palmer landscape – a haunt of ancient peace.

Oak Avenue, Keepers Cottage
Allan Pollock-Morris

Helmingham Hall, Suffolk, England, UK
Digital image shot on Nikon D2X

Nurtured Gardens
Judge's Favourite

Rusting Barn in Winter Landscape
Andy Phillipson

Jedburgh, Scottish Borders, Scotland, UK
Digital image shot on Canon EOS 350D

Nature's Garden

Ancient Tools ❷
Derek St Romaine

Royal Botanic Gardens, Kew, Surrey, England, UK
Colour transparency shot on Mamiya RZ Pro TL

Royal Botanic Gardens, Kew

Nothing is so beautiful in spring –
When weeds, in wheels, shoot
long and lovely and lush

GERARD MANLEY HOPKINS

EXTRACT FROM SPRING

Wild Tulip Duet – *Tulipa acuminita* 3
Carol Sharp

RHS Chelsea Flower Show, London, England, UK
Colour transparency shot on Nikon FM2

Nurtured Gardens

Gardening on Rapa Nui
Jeff Overs

Ahu Tongariki, Rapa Nui National Park, Easter Island, Chile
Digital image shot on Nikon D100

World Heritage Sites

Meadow at Great Dixter
Jonathan Buckley

Great Dixter, Rye, East Sussex, England, UK
Colour transparency shot on Nikon F100

Nurtured Gardens

May Woodlands
Tony Jones

Slindon Woods, West Sussex, England, UK
Colour transparency shot on Canon EOS 5

Nature's Garden

Frosty Foerster
Gary Rogers

Karl Foerster's Garden, Bornim, Potsdam, Germany
Colour transparency shot on Nikon F3

Nurtured Gardens

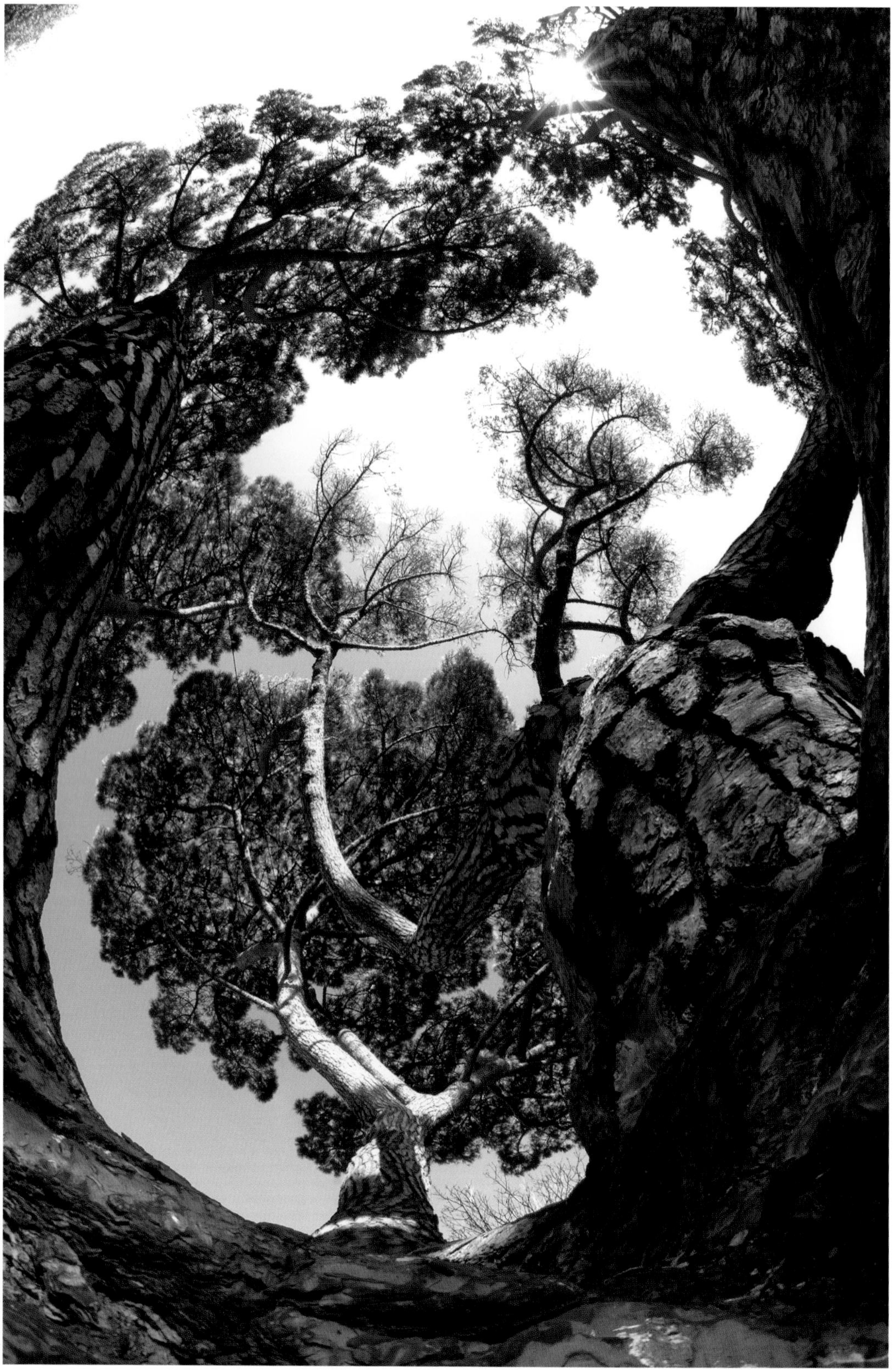

Ancient Landscape
John Garrett

Colorado National Park, Colorado, USA
Black and white negative shot on Nikon F5

Nature's Garden

Stone Pine
David Steel

Royal Botanic Gardens, Kew,
Surrey, England, UK
Digital image shot on Nikon D2X

Royal Botanic Gardens, Kew

3 **Winter at Mayhill**
Steve Gallagher

Mayhill, Gloucestershire, England, UK
Digital image shot on Canon EOS-1Ds Mark II

Nature's Garden

The Waterlily House – Out of Time
Michel Laverret

Royal Botanic Gardens, Kew, Surrey, England, UK
Colour negative shot on Canon EOS 50

Royal Botanic Gardens, Kew

The Sussex Downs
Charlie Hopkinson

Sussex, England, UK
Polaroid film shot on NPC land camera

Nature's Garden

White Campion
Pernilla Bergdahl

Wild Flower Meadow, Hampshire, Alresford, England, UK
Black and white negative, sepia toned shot on Pentax 67 II

Nature's Garden

Misty Morning at Kew
Steve Bicknell

Royal Botanic Gardens, Kew, Surrey, England, UK
Digital image shot on Canon EOS-1Ds Mark 1

Royal Botanic Gardens, Kew

Midsummer Dawn
Nicola Stocken Tomkins

Red Oaks, Redhill, Surrey, England, UK
Colour transparency shot on Hasselblad 503CXi

Nurtured Gardens

2 Orchid Beach
Peter Mason

Fraser Island, Queensland, Australia
Colour negative shot on Hasselblad 503CW

World Heritage Sites

Dead Heads
Steve Bicknell

Royal Botanic Gardens, Kew, Surrey, England, UK
Digital image shot on Canon EOS-1Ds Mark 1

Royal Botanic Gardens, Kew

Natural Curves
John Garrett

Photographer's Studio, London, England, UK
Black and white negative shot on Hasselblad 501 CM

Nurtured Gardens

Pond in Finland
Nadege Meriau

Near Pori, Satakunta, Finland
Colour negative shot on Hasselblad 500CM

Nature's Garden
Judge's Favourite

Judge's Favourite

Michael Hoppen
Michael Hoppen Gallery, UK

I was immediately drawn to this entry. In fact, the style was
so distinctive that I noticed several other images in different
categories that were by the same photographer. Each image
showed the same sensitivity to changing light and a time and
place. The images, especially this one, spoke of an intimate
silence that perfectly reflects the pleasure of walking
through nature.

The colour palette is perfectly controlled and also adopts an
unusual viewpoint. The image draws a miniature landscape
that examines the richness and diversity of nature in its raw
state. I would personally like to own this image so I could
look at it every day.`

Cliff Flora
Andrew Lawson

Marsland Mouth, Devon, England, UK
Colour transparency shot on Hasselblad XPan

Nature's Garden

Tree Shadows
Derek Harris

Sandringham House, Norfolk, England, UK
Colour transparency shot on Fuji
Panoramic GX 617

Nurtured Gardens

112

Parliament Square
Charlie Hopkinson

Westminster, London, England, UK
Polaroid film shot on NPC land camera

Nature's Garden

**No Future: Red Finale for the Old
Maple Tree in a Tokyo Tea Garden**
Tomoko Suzuki

Nichi-Nichi-An Private Tea Garden, Tokyo, Japan
Colour negative shot on Nikon F3

World Heritage Sites

The River Lee, Hackney Marshes
Dean Hollowood

River Lee, Hackney Marshes, London, England, UK
Colour negative shot on Mamiya RZ

Nature's Garden

Bad Hair Day
Andrew Butler

Royal Botanic Gardens, Kew, Surrey, England, UK
Digital image shot on Nikon D70

Royal Botanic Gardens, Kew

Useless Trees
Eduard Popescu

Ciucas Massif, Carpathian Mountains, Romania
Colour negative shot on Zenit-E

Nature's Garden

117

Spiral Staircase
Jeff Eden

Royal Botanic Gardens, Kew, Surrey, England, UK
Colour transparency shot on Nikon FM2

Royal Botanic Gardens, Kew

Treelines – Mapping Kew
Susan Bell

Royal Botanic Gardens, Kew, Surrey, England, UK
Colour transparency, polaroid transfer shot on Nikon F100

Royal Botanic Gardens, Kew

Amaryllis Papillon
Susan Bell

Photographer's Garden, London, England, UK
Colour transparency, polaroid transfer shot on Nikon F100

Nurtured Gardens

120

Wild at Heart #1
Dianna Jazwinski

Knoll Gardens, Dorset, England, UK
Colour transparency shot on Bronica ETR-Si

Nurtured Gardens

Val d'Orcia at Dawn
Mike Curry

Val d'Orcia, Tuscany, Italy
Digital image shot on Olympus E-1

World Heritage Sites

Agave 1
Jane Eaton Hamilton

Private Garden, Vancouver, British Columbia, Canada
Digital image shot on Canon-1Ds Mark II

Nurtured Gardens

Pettifers Dawn No. 3
Clive Nichols

Pettifers, Lower Wardington, Oxfordshire, England, UK
Digital image shot on Canon EOS-1Ds Mark II

Nurtured Gardens

Winter Morning
Kim Williams

Near Ludlow, Shropshire, England, UK
Black and white negative shot on Wista Field 45DX

Nature's Garden

Evening Sunlight
Kathy Collins

River Earn, Perthshire, Scotland, UK
Colour transparency shot on Fuji Panoramic GX 617

Nature's Garden

Index of Photographers

52
Jill Furmanovsky
13 The Dove Centre
109 Bartholomew Road
London
NW5 2BJ
England
UK
M: +44 (0)7976 329055
T: +44 (0)20 7267 4716
jfurmanovsky@yahoo.co.uk
www.jillfurmanovsky.co.uk

98
Steve Gallagher
83 Leonard Street
London
EC2A 4QS
England
UK
M: +44 (0)7832 249861
T: +44 (0)020 7729 1356
stevegallagher03@yahoo.co.uk
www.stevegallagher.com

61, 83, 97, 107
John Garrett
1 Amor Road
London
W6 0AN
England
UK
T: +44 (0)20 8932 7719
jr.garrett@virgin.net

84
Paul Green
34 Tetbury Street
Minchinhampton
Stroud
Gloucestershire
GL6 9JH
England
UK
T: +44 (0)7970 434312
paulgreen.minch@btopenworld.com

33
Anne Green-Armytage
Quince Farm
Spring Lane
Yaxham
Dereham
Norfolk
NR19 1SA
England
UK
T: +44 (0)1362 694223
anne@annegreenarmytage.com
www.annegreenarmytage.com

24, 35, 111
Derek Harris
4 Wakerley Court
Wakerley
Oakham
Rutland
LE15 8NZ
England
UK
T: +44 (0)1572 747588
F: +44 (0)1572 747409
derekharris.photography@virgin.net
www.derekharris-photography.com

115
Dean Hollowood
23 Northchurch Road
London
N1 4ED
England
UK
T: +44 (0)20 7249 7854
dean@deanandjohn.com

18, 100, 112
Charlie Hopkinson
M: +44 (0)7976 402 891
info@charliehopkinson.com
www.charliehopkinson.com

77
Jason Ingram
Unit 2
Cotswold Road
Bristol
BS3 4NL
England
UK
T: +44 (0)1179 663872
info@jasoningramphotographer.co.uk
www.jasoningram.co.uk

62, 68
Rowan Isaac
72 Church Road
Winterbourne Down
Bristol
BS36 1BY
England
UK
T: +44 (0)1454 777717
rowphot@aol.com
www.rowanisaac.com

38, 78, 120
Dianna Jazwinski
9 Merrion Court
55 Bournemouth Road
Poole
Dorset
BH14 0EN
England
UK
M: +44 (0)7956 366135
T: +44 (0)1202 723511
dijazwinski@fizzphotos.com
www.fizzphotos.com

94
Tony Jones
12 Warnham Road
Goring-by-Sea
West Sussex
BN12 4LL
England
UK
M: +44 (0)7800 635398
T: +44 (0)1903 246877

21, 44, 47, 48
Andrea Jones
316 Kew Road
Kew Gardens
Richmond
Surrey
TW9 3DU
England
UK
T: +44 (0)20 8287 0600
F: +44 (0)20 8287 0606
andrea@andreajones.co.uk
www.andreajones.co.uk

99
Michel Laverret
Le Murger Savoie B
Dreux
28100
France
T: +33 2 37 46 54 73
michel.laverret@wanadoo.fr

23, 110
Andrew Lawson
Noah's Ark
Market Street
Charlbury
Oxford
Oxfordshire
OX7 3PL
England
UK
T: +44 (0)1608 810654
F: +44 (0)1608 811251
photos@andrewlawson.com
www.andrewlawson.com

29, 40, 50, 79
Nadia Mackenzie
43 Palmerston Road
London
SW14 7QA
England
UK
M: +44 (0)7831 284473
T: +44 (0)20 8876 2664
F: +44 (0)20 8876 2664
nadia@nadiamackenzie.com
www.nadiamackenzie.com

26
John Martin
39 Newton Close
Walsgrave
Coventry
West Midlands
CV2 2FX
England
UK
M: +44 (0)7714 442239
T: +44 (0)24 7672 1499
john.martin_photos@btopenworld.com
www.fotoflora.com

104
Peter Mason
10 Cranleigh Mews
London
SW11 2QL
M: +44 (0)7774 496414
T: +44 (0)20 7738 9955
peter@petermason.biz
www.petermason.biz

27, 55, 108
Nadege Meriau
12a Carysfort Road
London
N16 9AL
England
UK
M: +44 (0)7966 395542
nadege@nadege.co.uk

19
George Munday
Ballydowane East
Bunmahon
Kilmacthomas
Co Waterford
Ireland
T: +353 51 292246
F: +353 51 292020
george@coppercoastworkshops.com
www.coppercoastworkshops.com

PRIVATEPLACES

128

51, 74, 123
Clive Nichols
Rickyard Barn
Castle Farm
Chacombe
Banbury
Oxon
OX17 2EN
England
UK
T: +44 (0)1295 712288
F: +44 (0)1295 713672
clive@clivenichols.com
www.clivenichols.com

41, 92
Jeff Overs
Garden Flat
68 Parkhill Road
London
NW3 2YT
England
UK
M: +44 (0)7860 705908
jeff.overs@bbc.co.uk
www.jeffovers.com

42
Sharon Pearson
74 Tressillian Road
London
SE4 1YD
England
UK
T: +44 (0)208 691 2310
sharon@sharonpearson.co.uk
www.sharonpearson.co.uk

88
Andy Phillipson
54 Farquhar Terrace
South Queensferry
Edinburgh
EH30 9RW
Scotland
UK
M: +44 (0)7968 738191
andy@livewireimage.com
www.livewireimage.com

31, 87
Allan Pollock-Morris
2nd Floor
145-147 St John Street
London
EC1V 4PY
England
UK
M: +44 (0)7788 411251
ap-m@ap-m.com
www.ap-m.com

116
Eduard Popescu
40 Rampayne Street
Longleat House
London
SW1V 2GT
England
UK
M: +44 (0)7737 979394
ed@just-looking.net
www.just-looking.net

95
Gary Rogers
Hogweg 9
22085 Hamburg
Germany
M: +49 172 429 5030
T: +49 40 229 8674
F: +49 40 229 8674
garyrfoto@aol.com
www.garyrogers-photo.com

49
Kevin Schafer
2148 Halleck Ave SW
Seattle
WA 98116
USA
T: +1 206 933 1668
kevin@kevinschafer.com
www.kevinschafer.com

91
Carol Sharp
71 Leonard Street
London
EC2A 4QU
England
UK
M: +44 (0)7802 183723
T: +44 (0)20 7729 8040
carol@carolsharp.co.uk
www.carolsharp.co.uk

89
Derek St Romaine
239a Hook Road
Chessington
Surrey
KT9 1EQ
England
UK
T: +44 (0)20 8397 3761
derek@gardenphotolibrary.com
www.gardenphotolibrary.com

96
David Steel
Flat 6
58 Lambs Conduit Street
London
WC1N 3LW
England
UK
M: +44 (0)7725 047537
T: +44 (0)20 7242 5373
david37steel@gmail.com
www.davidsteelimages.com

72
Lindsey Stock
54 Perspective
100 Westminster Bridge Road
London
SE1 7XA
England
UK
M: +44 (0)7970 588331
T: +44 (0)20 7928 4567
lindsey.stock@btconnect.com
www.stockshoots.co.uk

103
Nicola Stocken Tomkins
Halliford Studios
Manygate Lane
Shepperton
TW17 9EG
England
UK
T: +44 (0)1932 230990
nicola@gardenpix.co.uk
www.gardenpix.co.uk

113
Tomoko Suzuki
Agent: Tiffany Radmore
Vital Arts
1st Floor, 9 Prescot Street
London
E1 8PR
UK
T: +44 (0)20 7480 4654
eastandwest@mbi.nifty.com

20
David Tarn
7 Ragworth Place
Norton
Stockton-on-Tees
County
TS20 1EL
England
UK
T: +44 (0)1642 556771
david@davidtarn.com
www.davidtarn.com

70
Henrietta Van den Bergh
Church House
Broadway
Ilminster
Somerset
TA19 9RB
England
UK
M: +44 (0)7973 838452
info@hvdbphoto.com
www.hvdbphoto.com

60, 69, 82
Rob Whitworth
1 Test Cottages
St Mary Bourne
Andover
Hampshire
SP11 6BX
England
UK
M: +44 (0)7880 733027
T: +44 (0)1264 738074
F: +44 (0)1264 738074
rob.whitworth@virgin.net

124
Kim Williams
10 The Quarry
Betchworth
Surrey
RH3 7BY
England
UK
M: +44 (0)7929 728562
T: +44 (0)1737 844068
kimhelen@stigs.demon.co.uk